DISCOVER
The Life Cycle of Bees

by Carol Pugliano-Martin

Table of Contents

Introduction 2
Chapter 1 What Is the Life Cycle of Bees? 4
Chapter 2 Where Do Bees Live? 8
Chapter 3 What Do Nests Have? 12
Conclusion 18
Concept Map 20
Glossary 22
Index 24

Introduction

Living things have **life cycles**. **Bees** have a life cycle.

▲ Bees are living.

Words to Know

 bees

 hives

 larvae

 life cycles

 nests

 pupae

See the Glossary on page 22.

Chapter 1

What Is the Life Cycle of Bees?

Bees are eggs first.

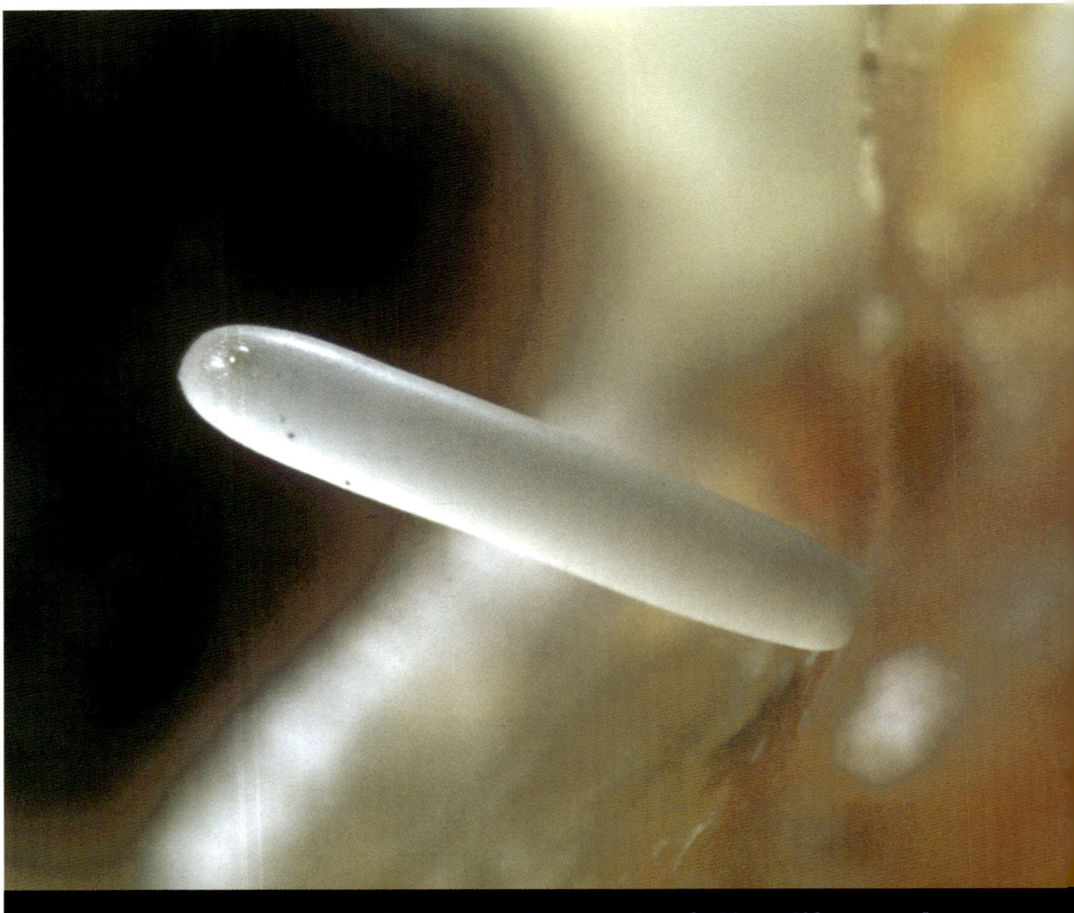

▲ An egg is part of the life cycle.

It's a Fact
Bees hatch from eggs.

Bees are **larvae** next.

▲ Larvae are part of the life cycle.

Chapter 1

Bees are **pupae** next.

▲ Pupae are part of the life cycle.

What Is the Life Cycle of Bees?

Bees are young next.

▲ Young bees are part of the life cycle.

Bees are adults at last.

▲ An adult bee is part of the life cycle.

Chapter 2

Where Do Bees Live?

Bees live in **hives**.

▲ Bees live in this hive.

Bees live in tree **nests**.

▲ Bees live in this nest.

Chapter 2

Bees live in leaf nests.

▲ Bees live in this nest.

Where Do Bees Live?

Bees live in ground nests.

▲ Bees live in this nest.

It's a Fact
Some bees live under buildings.

Chapter 3

What Do Nests Have?

Nests have eggs.

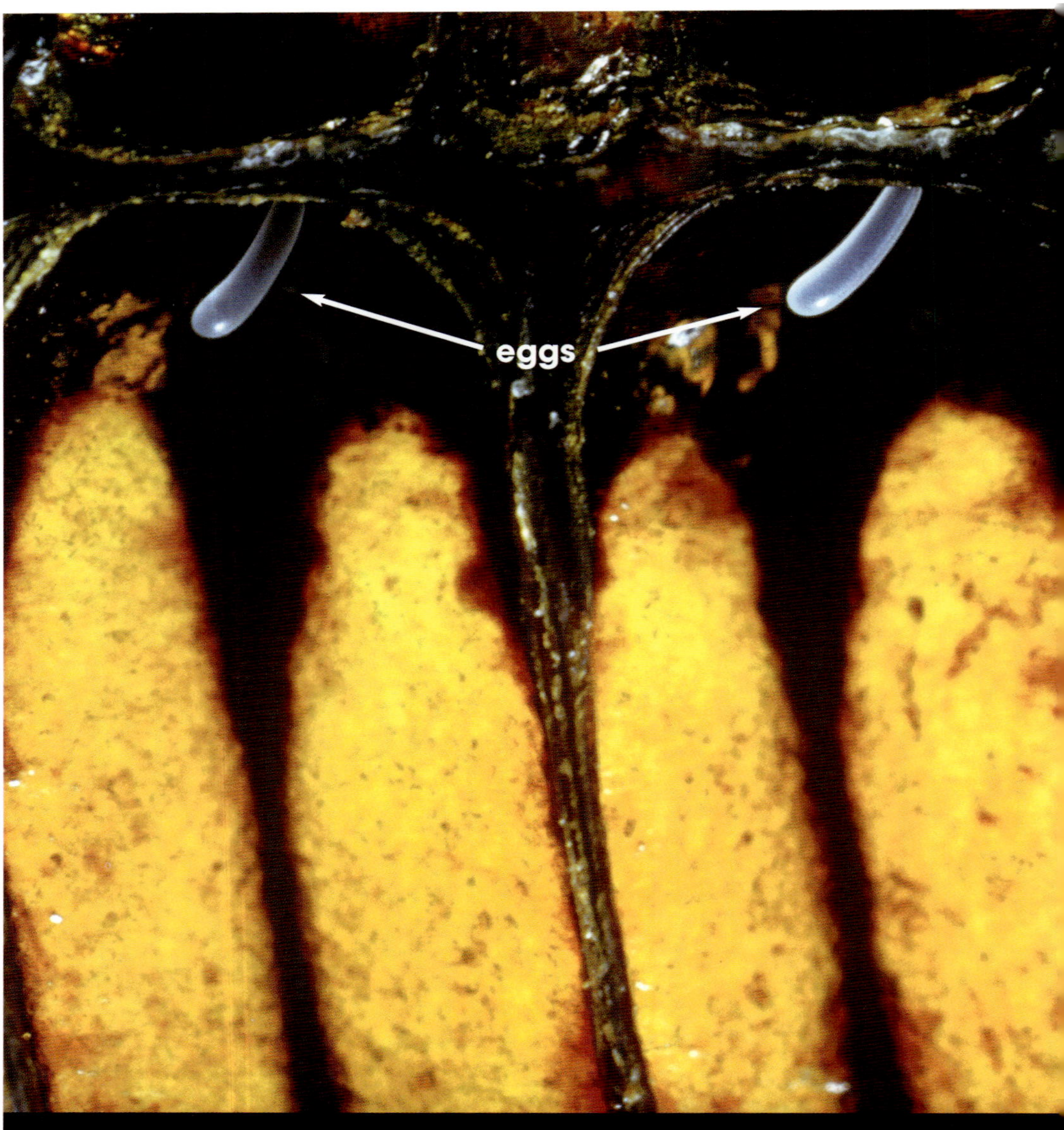

▲ Eggs are in the nest.

Nests have larvae.

▲ Larvae are in the nest.

Chapter 3

Nests have pupae.

▲ Pupae are in the nest.

Nests have young bees.

▲ Young bees are in the nest.

What Do Nests Have?

Nests have a queen bee.

▲ A queen bee is in the nest.

It's a Fact
Queen bees lay eggs.

Chapter 3

Nests have female bees. Nests have worker bees.

▲ A female bee is in the nest.

What Do Nests Have?

Nests have male bees.

▲ Male bees are in the nest.

Conclusion

Bees have a life cycle.

▲ All bees have a life cycle.

Concept Map

The Life Cycle of Bees

What Is the Life Cycle of Bees?

- eggs first
- larvae next
- pupae next
- young bees next
- adult bees last

Where Do Bees Live?

- hives
- tree nests
- leaf nests
- ground nests

What Do Nests Have?

eggs
larvae
pupae
young bees
queen bee
female bees
male bees

Glossary

bees insects that collect pollen and nectar

Bees have a life cycle.

hives homes for bees

Bees live in **hives**.

larvae small creatures that become bees

Bees are **larvae** next.

life cycles stages in the life of an organism

Living things have **life cycles**.

nests places bees live

Bees live in tree **nests**.

pupae larvae in cocoons

Bees are **pupae** next.

Index

bees, 2, 4–11, 14–18
eggs, 4, 12
hives, 8
larvae, 5, 13
life cycles, 2, 18
nests, 9–17
pupae, 6, 14